WITHDRAWN
Woodridge Public Library

	Wright, Lynne.		
J	The science of		
534	noise		
Wri			

The Science of Noise

Lynne Wright

RSVP
RAINTREE
STECK-VAUGHN
P U B L I S H E R S
A Steck-Vaughn Company

Austin, Texas

www.steck-vaughn.com

Science World

Other titles in the series:

The Science of
Gravity

The Science of a
Light Bulb

The Science of a
Spring

Picture acknowledgments
The publishers would like to thank the following for allowing their pictures to be reproduced in this book: Ace/Patrick Blake 5 (top), /Geoff du Feu 22 (middle), /Ray Spence 5 (bottom); Bubbles/Vicki Bonomo 16 (top), /Ian West 26, /Jennie Woodcock 19 (top); Martyn F. Chillmaid 10 (both), 28 (top), 29 (bottom); Eye Ubiquitous 18, 21 (bottom), /Roger Chester 16 (bottom), NASA 14; Image Bank 23; Getty Images cover [inset top], 23 (top), /Lonnie Duka 17, /Robert Frerck 27 (top), 29 (top), /Bruno de Hogues 25; /Tom Main cover [inset center], /Art Wolfe 22 (bottom); Robert Harding 4 (bottom), /Louise Murray 21 (middle); Image Bank 23 (bottom); Science Photo Library/Crown Copyright/Health and Safety laboratory 15 (top), /Tim Davis 21 (top), Richard Megna 24; /Dr Morley Read 19 (bottom); Wayland Picture Library cover [main], title page, contents page, 5 (middle), 7–9, 11, 15 (bottom), 20, 22, 26, 27 (bottom), 28 (bottom), /Chris Fairclough 4 (top); Zefa 12.
Illustrator: Peter Bull

Published by Raintree Steck-Vaughn Publishers, an imprint of Steck-Vaughn Company

Printed in Italy. Bound in the United States.
1 2 3 4 5 6 7 8 9 0 04 03 02 01 00

Library of Congress Cataloging-in-Publication Data
Wright, Lynne.
The science of noise / Lynne Wright.
    p.   cm.—(Science world)
Includes bibliographical references and index.
Summary: Describes different sounds, how they are made, how they travel, and how to change sounds by altering the pitch or volume.
ISBN 0-7398-1324-2
1. Sound—Juvenile literature.
[1. Sound.]
I. Title. II. Series.
QC225.5.W75 2000
534—dc21   99-37304

Contents

Where Does Sound Come From?

There are sounds all around us. Listen, right now, where you are. What can you hear? How many different sounds can you hear? What is making each noise? If you went to another place, would you hear the same or other sounds? Listen next time you are in a busy place, such as a store or city. What sounds are around you? If you go into a park or a forest, do you hear even more sounds?

▲ What sounds would you hear if you were near these cows in the country?

◀ What sounds would you hear if you were near this busy road?

Think of all the sounds you can hear, or that you know. Are they all equally loud or equally quiet, or are they different? Are they high sounds or low sounds, or a mixture? Are they all pleasant sounds, or don't you like some of them? What is your favorite sound? Are there any sounds you don't like? Do you know why this is?

▲ What sounds do you think you would hear in the country?

◀ What sounds do you think you would hear in a park?

Describing sounds

Sounds can be described as noisy or musical. Noise can be tiring or irritating. If it is very loud, it can harm our ears. A musical sound can also be loud. But because it is made in a different way from noise, it is usually more pleasant to listen to.

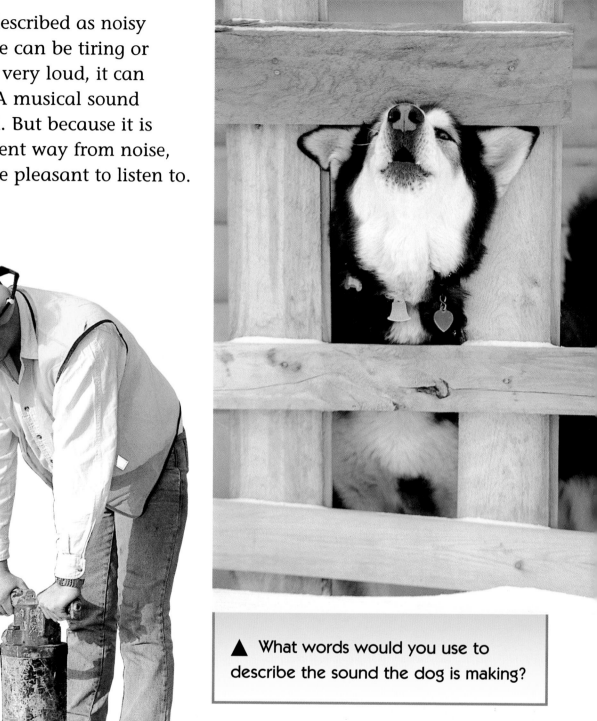

▲ What words would you use to describe the sound the dog is making?

◄ What words would you use to describe the sounds this man is making?

What are decibels?

We measure how loud sounds are in decibels. A whisper measures about 12 decibels. A sound of 120 decibels can hurt your ears. A jet engine 100 ft. (30 m) away makes a sound of about 140 decibels.

◄ What words would you use to describe the sea?

You could sort the sounds you hear into different groups. Arrange loud sounds and soft sounds, or sounds made by machines and sounds made naturally. Think of some other ways to sort the sounds that you know.

What words ► would you use to describe a lawn mower?

There are many different ways you can make sounds

You could clap your hands, hum, rattle a box of pasta, or pull on a rubber band. Which sounds are made by shaking, like a tambourine? Which are made by picking, like a guitar? Which are made by banging, like a drum? Are any made by blowing, like a whistle? Are there other ways to make sounds, such as scratching and rubbing?

Do you think all these sounds would be equally loud? Or would some be quieter than others? Would some sounds be higher than others, or lower? Would they have the same pitch?

Vibrations

Put your fingers lightly halfway up your throat. When you start to talk, you will feel your voice box moving. When you stop talking, it will stop moving. These motions are called vibrations. Animals also make vibrations when they make noises such as barking or purring.

▲ Which part of the cat is vibrating to make the purring sound?

What vibrates when you make your own sounds?

How can we be sure that sound is made when something vibrates? Stretch a rubber band across one hand and pick it with the other hand. We can see and feel the vibrations, and hear the noise.

◄ Hold a ruler flat on a tabletop so that most of it is sticking out. It is not moving, and there is no sound. Now bang down on the free end with your other hand. The ruler makes a sound, and you can see the free part moving. It is vibrating.

Put some grains of rice on a piece of stiff ► paper. Hold it above a drum, not touching it. Ask a friend to bang the drum, and you can watch the rice grains move. When your friend bangs the drum, the drumskin vibrates. The vibrations flow out into the air around the drum. They make the paper and rice grains vibrate, too.

What happens when you blow across the top of an empty bottle? There is sound coming from the bottle, but the bottle is not vibrating. It is the air inside it. Get a few bottles that are alike and fill them with different amounts of water. They will make different sounds.

▼ The bottle with the longest column of air in it will make the deeper sound. Which one will make the highest sound?

What are wind instruments?

Wind instruments are instruments that have one or several tubes of air. A player blows down a tube, the air vibrates, and a musical sound is made. There are many different wind instruments, including recorders, flutes, clarinets, tubas, and panpipes. All have different ways of making sounds. For example, you blow down a recorder using its shaped mouthpiece, and you blow across the top of a panpipe tube in the same way that you blow across the top of a bottle.

How Does Sound Travel?

An object needs to vibrate for there to be a sound. But how does the sound get from the object to our ears? How do we hear someone clapping his or her hands across the room?

◄ As hands clap, the vibration of the hands makes the air surrounding them vibrate, too. These vibrations travel through the air until they get weak and die away. The vibrations are known as sound waves. These waves travel outward in all directions from the vibrating object.

Different objects send out different sound waves. The sound waves vibrate at different rates. The pitch of the sound made depends on the number of vibrations per second. The more vibrations there are per second, the higher the sound.

We hear sounds with our ears. The part of the ear outside the head is only the start of the hearing chain. It works like a funnel, a small tube with a wide mouth. It allows the sound waves to go down it to the inner ear inside the head. When they reach the eardrum, it vibrates the sound waves along to the inner ear, which sends messages to the brain. The brain then works out what we hear.

▼ This diagram shows how sound travels to our ears.

2. The sound waves travel along this tube called the auditory canal.

3. The eardrum vibrates when a sound wave hits it.

4. The vibrating eardrum makes the little bones vibrate.

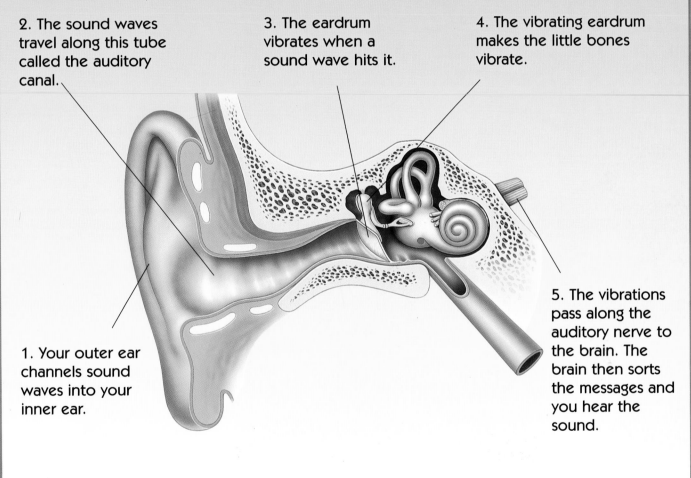

5. The vibrations pass along the auditory nerve to the brain. The brain then sorts the messages and you hear the sound.

1. Your outer ear channels sound waves into your inner ear.

Some sounds don't vibrate with enough energy to make the eardrums vibrate. And we can't hear these sounds. Some sounds have so much energy that they hurt our ears. The more energy, the louder the sound.

Does sound travel only through the air?

If you are outside, you hear sounds in the same area you are in. If you are inside, you hear sounds in the same room you are in. However, you can also hear sounds coming from other rooms. How do these sounds travel to you if there are walls and doors in the way?

How fast does sound travel?

Sound travels at about 1,087 ft. (330 m) per second. Light travels almost a million times faster than sound, at 186,000 mi. (300,000 km) per second.

Sound travels through other materials, not just air. So it will travel through the wood of a door and the glass of a window. All materials are made up of tiny bits called particles, which vibrate.

◄ In space there are no air particles, and so there is no sound.

Where there is nothing, not even air, there is no sound. This is called a vacuum. Sound will not travel through a vacuum because there are no particles to vibrate.

Some sounds, such ▶ as an explosion, are loud enough to hurt the ears. A blast has about 5 million times as much energy as a voice whispering!

Sounds travel more quickly through solid materials, such as wood, than through liquids, such as water. This is true because the particles are closer together in solids. Liquids carry sound better than gases, such as air, where the particles are spread out more. Next time you are at a swimming pool try talking to a friend underwater. Notice how loud your voices sound. Is the sound clear?

Ask a friend to tap a tabletop with his or her fingers. ▶ Put your head down on the table. Does the sound seem louder with your head on or off the table?

Stopping sounds

Can you think of times when you don't want to hear anything? When you are trying to go to sleep, you might pull a blanket over your ears. That blocks out sounds. When you are thinking about something you are doing, you don't want to be disturbed by noise. You might put your fingers in your ears. Doing these things keeps the sound waves from entering your ears.

Sound travels better through some materials than others. So some materials are better at keeping out the sounds we don't want to hear.

▲ Covering your ears against noise blocks out sounds.

Double-paned windows are made of two sheets of glass with a vacuum in between them. Sound can't travel through the vacuum, and so the room is quieter. Most noise will not travel through, but not all the noise is kept out. Some sounds will travel through the window frames and the walls.

Some buildings near busy ▶ roads, airports, or other noisy places have double-paned windows. They keep a lot of sounds from coming in from the outside.

Which materials keep out sound best?

The materials that are better at keeping out the sounds are soft ones. They contain pockets of air. Air is not as good at passing on vibrations as solid materials. For that reason the sound seems quieter when it reaches our ears.

Some jobs require special ear guards to keep loud sounds from harming workers' ears. You will see people wearing ear guards on building sites and runways at airports. They are also worn in factories where there are noisy machines.

▼ This carpenter is wearing ear guards while he works to block out the sound of the loud machines.

Some places need to be especially quiet for a purpose, such as recording studios and radio stations. They need to be soundproofed so that outside noises don't spoil a broadcast or finished recording. The walls are made of special materials that keep noise out and will not cause echoes.

Echoes

Echoes are made when sound bounces off smooth, hard surfaces such as wooden floors and walls. This is one reason we put carpets on the floor and wallpaper on the walls.

◀ Toys banged on a carpeted floor will make less noise than toys banged on a wooden floor. This is true because sound doesn't travel so well through carpets, and there are no echoes.

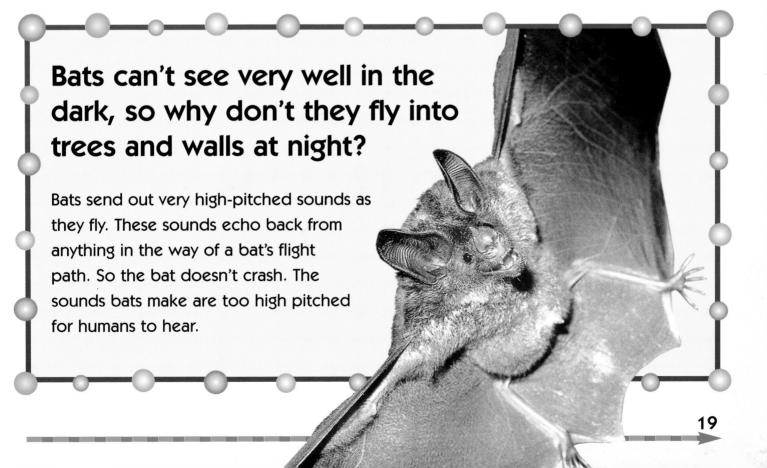

Bats can't see very well in the dark, so why don't they fly into trees and walls at night?

Bats send out very high-pitched sounds as they fly. These sounds echo back from anything in the way of a bat's flight path. So the bat doesn't crash. The sounds bats make are too high pitched for humans to hear.

How Do We Hear Sounds?

We hear with our ears. We have two ears, one on each side of the head. They allow us to say where a sound is coming from. Can you hear sounds equally well that are made in front of you, to one side, or behind you? We can hear around corners and through walls and doors. But we can't always see the places where the sounds come from.

◀ Put something over your eyes and cover one ear. Ask a friend to make a noise behind you. Can you figure out which direction the noise is coming from?

Why is it important that we are able to hear where sounds are coming from? If we could not do this, we would be in a lot of danger. We could not hear the direction traffic was coming from when we cross the road. We could not hear a warning shout to tell us we're in danger.

20

It is very important for some kinds of animals to hear well. Some animals, especially those that hunt at night, need to be able to listen for animals they hunt. Some animals, which don't feed on other animals, need to hear an animal hunting them.

An owl hunts at night and relies on its hearing ▶ to find its next meal. It hunts small animals, such as mice, and can find one in total darkness just by following a distant sound of rustling leaves.

▼ A lynx uses its good sense of hearing to help it find food.

▼ A rabbit needs to catch the quiet sounds of a hunting animal so that it can escape.

The lives of many animals depend upon having good hearing. Some animals, like zebras, have large, forward-facing ears that are very good at catching sounds. They turn their heads when they are listening. Other animals, such as cats, can move their ears separately to catch sounds around them. Dogs with floppy ears can make their ear flaps stand up when they hear a sound. By doing this they are making a bigger funnel to catch the sounds.

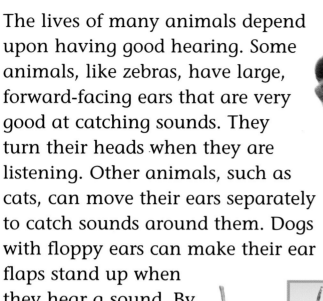

▲ Hamsters need to hear danger so they can run away.

A cheetah needs to hear well to find its next meal. ▼

◄ Insects don't have ears like ours. Some have holes in their bodies through which they can hear sounds. Some moths have small holes on the sides of their body, and crickets (left) have theirs on their front legs.

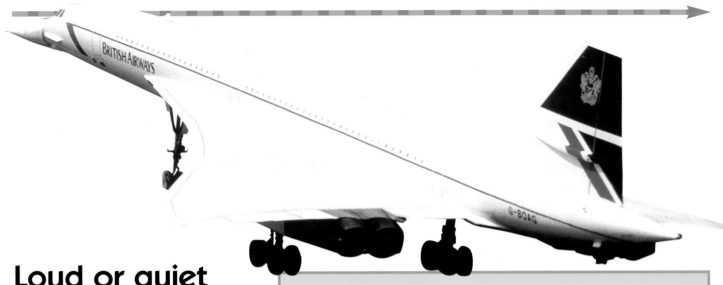

Loud or quiet

Try dropping a pencil box far away from people and then near to them. They will hear the sound differently, even though you made the same sound. Sounds seem louder the

▲ The Concorde travels faster than the speed of sound as it flies across the world's skies. It flies thousands of feet in the air. But the loud roar of its engines can clearly be heard above noise on the ground. Loud sounds can be heard farther away than quiet sounds. Loud sounds have more sound energy.

nearer you are to them. They seem quieter the farther away you are, even though they really are not. This happens because the sound waves from the vibrating object move out in every direction. The energy in these sound waves moves outward. It then spreads over a greater area, and it decreases. Less energy makes a quieter sound.

At times we want someone to hear us a long ▶ way away. We put our hands around our mouths, and make a funnel. It keeps the sound waves from spreading. So more of the sound energy travels in the direction you want it to.

How Can We Change Sound?

Next time you listen to some music notice how the sounds are different. They go from high to low. We use the word *pitch* to describe how high or low a sound is. Can you make high and low sounds with your voice? Start with a low-pitched sound. Then gradually go higher until you are making a high-pitched sound.

The pitch of a sound can be changed. The faster an object, or the air around it, vibrates, the higher the pitch.

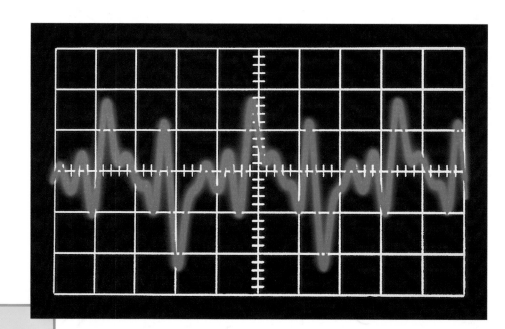

These sound waves ▶ show the pitch of a note made by a harmonica (top) and a recorder (bottom). The recorder holds a steadier note than the harmonica. Notice the recorder's steady and repeating sound-wave pattern.

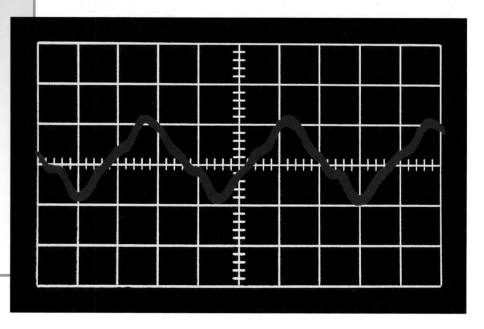

A drum is made of a skin stretched across a hoop of wood or metal. A drummer bangs the skin with his or her hand, or a stick. Then the skin vibrates to produce sound. A drummer can change the sound a drum makes. The skin across the hoop can be tightened. The tighter the skin, the higher the sound.

▲ You can see where the skins of these drums have been fastened around the hoop. The drums will all have a different pitch. It depends on how tight the skin on each drum is.

Stringed instruments, such as guitars and sitars, make sounds when the strings are picked. If the strings are loose, they will make lower sounds than if they are tight. The pitch of the sounds also depends on where the player places his or her fingers.

This boy is holding a stringed instrument called a ▶ sitar. It makes a low-pitched sound when picked. If he holds the strings against the sitar's neck, he shortens them. Then the pitch will be higher.

▼ When this player puts his finger high up on the string, the sound is low pitched. If he moves his finger down the string, the player will shorten it. Then the sound will be higher.

Wind instruments produce sounds when the player blows down a tube of air. This makes the air vibrate.

◀ Pan pipes have tubes of different sizes. So the columns of air are of different sizes. Which pipe will make the lowest sound? The longest pipe will make the lowest sound. The shortest pipe will make the highest sound.

A recorder is just one tube of air that the player blows down. The recorder has a row of holes down one side. The player covers the holes with his or her fingers. This changes the length of the column of air that will vibrate. When only one hole is covered, the recorder makes a low-pitched sound. When several holes are covered, the column of vibrating air is made shorter. Then a higher-pitched sound is made.

The player must cover all the holes on the ▶ recorder to produce the lowest sound. How will she make the highest sound?

Varying volumes

Sounds can also be of different volumes, loud or soft. The volume depends upon how much energy is put into making the sound. The more energy you put into a sound, by banging or blowing harder, the louder it is.

When you shout, you build up your breath ▶ to let it out in a mighty noise.

▼ When you whisper, you let less breath out, and you make less noise. You may also cup your hands around your mouth to direct the sound.

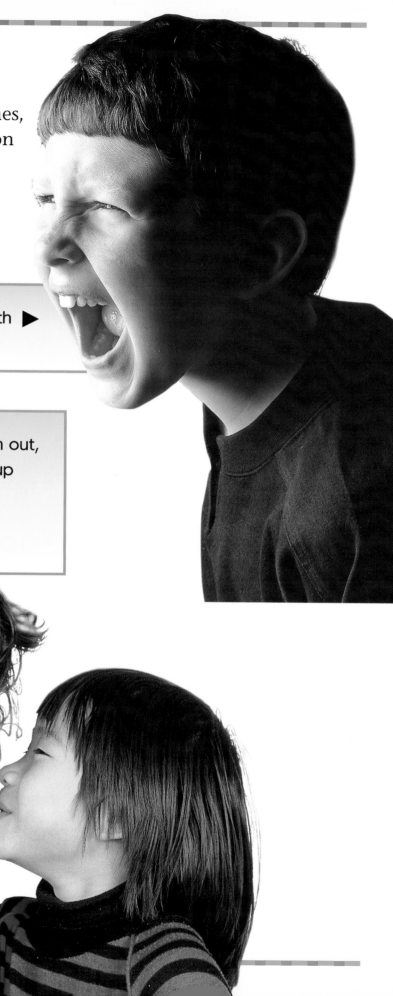

Some stringed ▶
instruments have a box
behind the strings. This makes
the sound louder. We say it
amplifies the sound.

Human ears find very
high and very low
sounds difficult to hear
well. Human ears can pick up
sound waves that vibrate up
to 20,000 times a second.

◀ Dogs can pick up
sound waves that
vibrate more than
30,000 times a
second. They can
hear high-pitched
sounds that we can't.

Glossary

Amplify Make a sound louder.

Auditory Having something to do with hearing.

Auditory canal The inside part of ear that sound waves are guided down from the outer ear. It connects to the eardrum.

Decibels The units for measuring how loud a sound is.

Eardrum A flap of skin separating the outside part of the ear from the inner ear.

Ears The sense organs that allow us to hear sounds.

Echoes Sounds that strike a smooth, hard surface, such as rock, and bounce back. They seem to be coming from in front of us.

Energy The power to make things work.

Music A type of sound made by an object sending out regular vibrations spaced at regular times, such as a guitar string.

Nerve The part of the body that sends messages to the brain.

Noise A type of sound made by an object sending out vibrations not spaced at regular times, such as a banging door.

Pitch The highness or lowness of a note. It depends upon the number of vibrations made every second.

Sound Any noise made by the vibrations of an object.

Soundproofed Protected against sound. Soundproofing is usually used to keep out unwanted sounds, such as traffic noise, or to stop echoes.

Sound waves Waves of vibrating air that transfer sound energy from a vibrating object to our ears.

Vacuum A space that has nothing in it, not even air particles.

Vibrations Rapid movements back and forth. Vibrations cause sound. Different objects vibrate at different speeds. The speed of vibration is measured in hertz (Hz) as the number of vibrations each second. One vibration is equal to one hertz.

Voice box The part of the body where vibrations are made in order to make sounds, i.e., the voice.

Further Information

Books to read

De Pinna, Simon. *Sound* (Science Projects). Austin, TX: Raintree Steck-Vaughn, 1998.

Grimshaw, Caroline. *Sound* (Invisible Journeys). Chicago: World Book, 1998.

Haslam, Andrew. *Sound* (Make It Work). New York: Scholastic, Inc., 1998.

Madgwick, Wendy. *Super Sound* (Science Starters). Austin, TX: Raintree Steck-Vaughn, 1999.

Parker, Steve. *Sound* (Science Works). Milwaukee, WI: Gareth Stevens, 1997.

Richard. Jon. *Sound and Music* (Science Factory). Brookfield, CT: Copper Beech Books, 1999.

Web sites to visit

ericir.syr.edu/Projects/Newton/newtonalpha This site contains many interesting science lessons.

www.lsc.org
This is the home page of the Liberty Science Center.

www.discoveryplace.org
This is the home page of Discovery Place.

www-hpcc.asto.washington.edu/ scied/ museum.html
This site has links to many science museums.

Places to visit

Liberty Science Center, Liberty State Park, Phillip Street, Jersey City, NJ (Tel: 201-200-1000). This outstanding science museum has hands-on activities guided by the museum staff.

Discovery Place, 301 North Tryon Street, Charlotte, NC (Tel: 1-800-935-0553). This is an award-winning science and technology museum, featuring hands-on experiments.

Index

Numbers in **bold** refer to pictures as well as text.